COUNTRY · EXPLORERS

A Visit to

THE NETHERLANDS

by Charis Mather

BEARPORT
PUBLISHING

Minneapolis, Minnesota

Credits

All images are courtesy of Shutterstock.com, unless otherwise specified. With thanks to Getty Images, Thinkstock Photo, and iStockphoto.

Cover – Dancake, FamVeld, Yasonya. 2-3 – Yasonya. 4-5 – Nerthuz, S-F. 6-7 – Yasonya, T. Lesia. 8-9 – Rudy Balasko, cla78. 10-11 – Nikolay Antonov, Ververidis Vasilis. 12-13 – rob3rt82, iPics. 14-15 – Raisa Suprun, Vitalinka. 16-17 – Jolanda Aalbers, www.hollandfoto.net. 18-19 – Andrii Lutsyk, TonyV3112. 20-21 – Alberto Loyo, Elena Pominova, 22-23 – Rudmer Zwerver, Yasonya.

Library of Congress Cataloging-in-Publication Data is available at www.loc.gov or upon request from the publisher.

ISBN: 979-8-88509-375-0 (hardcover)
ISBN: 979-8-88509-497-9 (paperback)
ISBN: 979-8-88509-612-6 (ebook)

© 2023 Booklife Publishing
This edition is published by arrangement with Booklife Publishing.

For more information, write to Bearport Publishing, 5357 Penn Avenue South, Minneapolis, MN 55419.

CONTENTS

COUNTRY TO COUNTRY

A country is an area of land marked by **borders**. The people in each country have their own rules and ways of living. They may speak different languages.

Which country do you live in?

4

Each country around the world has its own interesting things to see and do. Let's take a trip to visit a country and learn more!

Have you ever visited another country?

TODAY'S TRIP IS TO
THE NETHERLANDS!

The Netherlands

EUROPE

ASIA

NORTH
AMERICA

AFRICA

SOUTH
AMERICA

AUSTRALIA

The Netherlands is a country
in the **continent** of Europe.

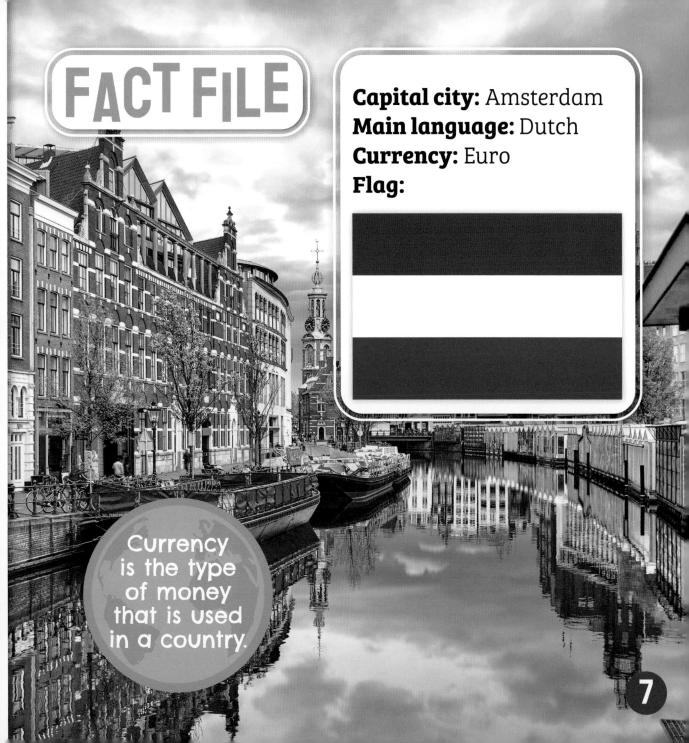

FACT FILE

Capital city: Amsterdam
Main language: Dutch
Currency: Euro
Flag:

Currency is the type of money that is used in a country.

ROTTERDAM

We'll start our trip in Rotterdam, one of the biggest cities in the Netherlands. Rotterdam has a large river that allows many boats to travel through the city.

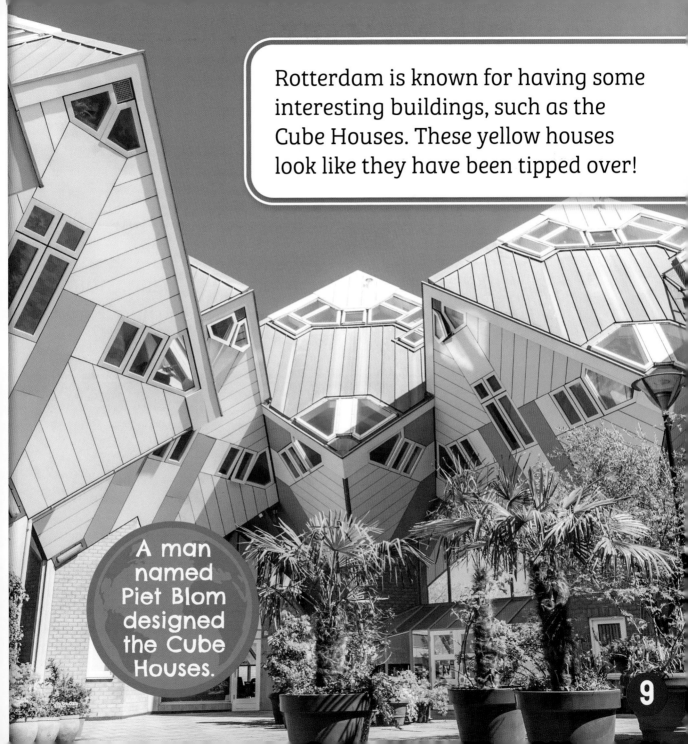

Rotterdam is known for having some interesting buildings, such as the Cube Houses. These yellow houses look like they have been tipped over!

A man named Piet Blom designed the Cube Houses.

9

KINDERDIJK WINDMILLS

The Netherlands is mostly flat, which means the land can easily **flood**. Hundreds of years ago, people found a way to stop flooding in the **village** of Kinderdijk. They built 19 windmills.

Windmill

These machines help move extra water off the land and into rivers. They can still work today! But they are a popular tourist spot, too.

GIETHOORN

The Netherlands has a lot of **canals**. The village of Giethoorn is known for using these waterways instead of roads. People there often travel by boat.

In the winter, the canals sometimes freeze over. Then, people in Giethoorn skate on the ice!

KEUKENHOF GARDENS

Next, we'll go see some flower gardens. The Keukenhof gardens are some of the largest in the world. They are filled with millions of colorful tulips.

Float made of flowers

In the spring, there is a flower parade in the gardens. It includes amazing **floats** covered with real flowers.

ART

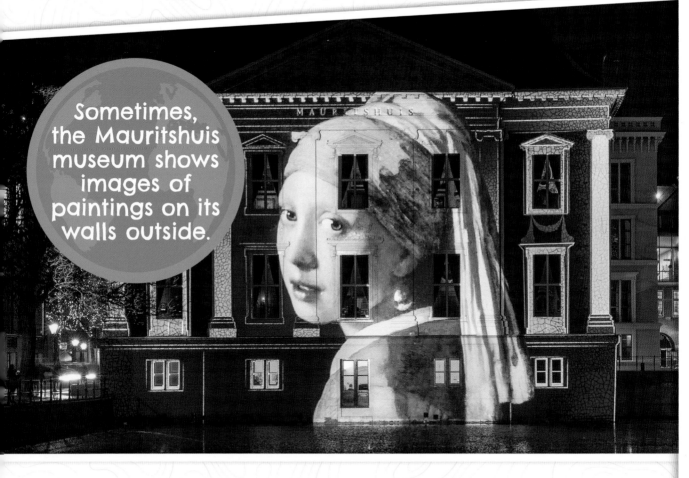

Sometimes, the Mauritshuis museum shows images of paintings on its walls outside.

We can find amazing things in the country's many art museums, too. Every year, millions of people visit to see the art.

The museums have a lot of paintings by famous Dutch artists, including Vincent van Gogh, Rembrandt, and Johannes Vermeer.

The word *Dutch* describes someone or something from the Netherlands.

van Gogh Museum

Amsterdam

BICYCLING

Let's go on a bike ride! Bicycling is a very common way to travel in the Netherlands. Many cities have roads just for people on bikes.

Sometimes, it's easier to get places by bike than by car. In busy cities, bicycles are everywhere.

19

CHEESE

Let's try some cheese! Dutch people have made this tasty snack for hundreds of years. Some towns even have special markets where cheese is sold in large, round blocks called wheels.

Sellers at these markets sometimes wear **traditional** clothing and carry the wheels on wooden **barrows**. People visit the cheese markets to taste the cheese and watch the people carrying it.

BEFORE YOU GO

We can't forget to visit De Hoge Veluwe National Park.
It's a great place to walk or bike through nature.
If we're lucky, we might see a few red deer.

We could also take a trip to Volendam. This fishing village has colorful wooden houses next to the **harbor**. While we're there, we can eat some delicious fish.

What have you learned about the Netherlands on this trip?

23

GLOSSARY

barrows wooden platforms for carrying goods, such as food

borders lines that show where one place ends and another begins

canals small waterways built for boat travel or to move water

continent one of the world's seven large land masses

floats large decorations used during a parade

flood to fill an area with lots of water

harbor an area of water along land where ships stay when not being used

traditional relating to something that a group of people has done for many years

village an area of houses and businesses that is smaller than a town and is usually located in the countryside

INDEX

24